MY SIDEWALKS ON
SCOTT FORESMAN
READING STREET

Reaching for Goals

Program Authors

Connie Juel, Ph.D.

Jeanne R. Paratore, Ed.D.

Deborah Simmons, Ph.D.

Sharon Vaughn, Ph.D.

Glenview, Illinois
Boston, Massachusetts
Chandler, Arizona
Hoboken, New Jersey

ISBN-13: 978-0-328-45291-0
ISBN-10:   0-328-45291-2

11 12 13 14 15 V011 18 17 16 15 14
CC1

Reaching for Goals

Opportunity Knocks

How can we be successful?

5

Challenges

31

How can we overcome obstacles
to reach our goals?

American Journeys

How can moving change our view of the world?

GRAND Gestures

When do people choose to make sacrifices?

Space

How do we reach for the stars?

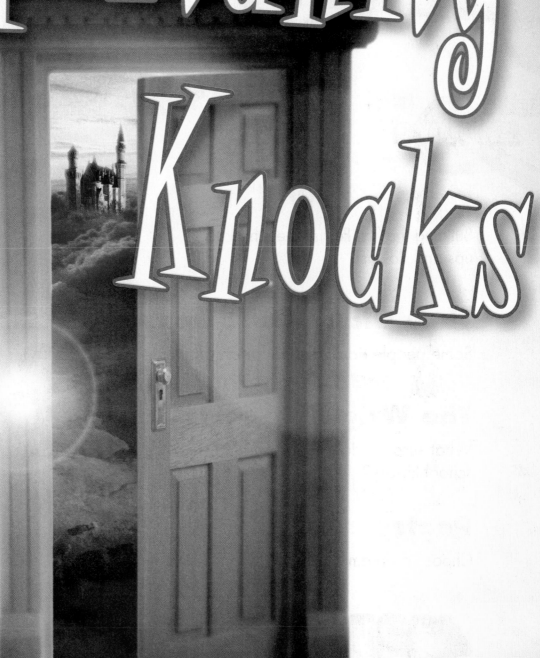

Opportunity Knocks

Contents

Opportunity Knocks

Let's Explore

6

Words 2 the Wise

Sometimes **opportunity knocks** when we least expect it. It could be a book, a person, or an event. As you read, think about opportunities you have had in your life.

THE FERRIS WHEEL

In 1892, the city of Chicago was selected to host a world's fair. Hosting the fair was an opportunity to show the world what a great city Chicago was. For the last world's fair, the city of Paris built the Eiffel Tower. Could Chicago build something as wonderful?

Many inventors suggested ideas. Then George Ferris suggested a 250-foot high wheel. The wheel would turn in a slow circle. Riders could look out over the entire fair.

1. George Ferris built bridges before building the Ferris wheel.

2. It cost 50 cents to ride on the Ferris wheel.

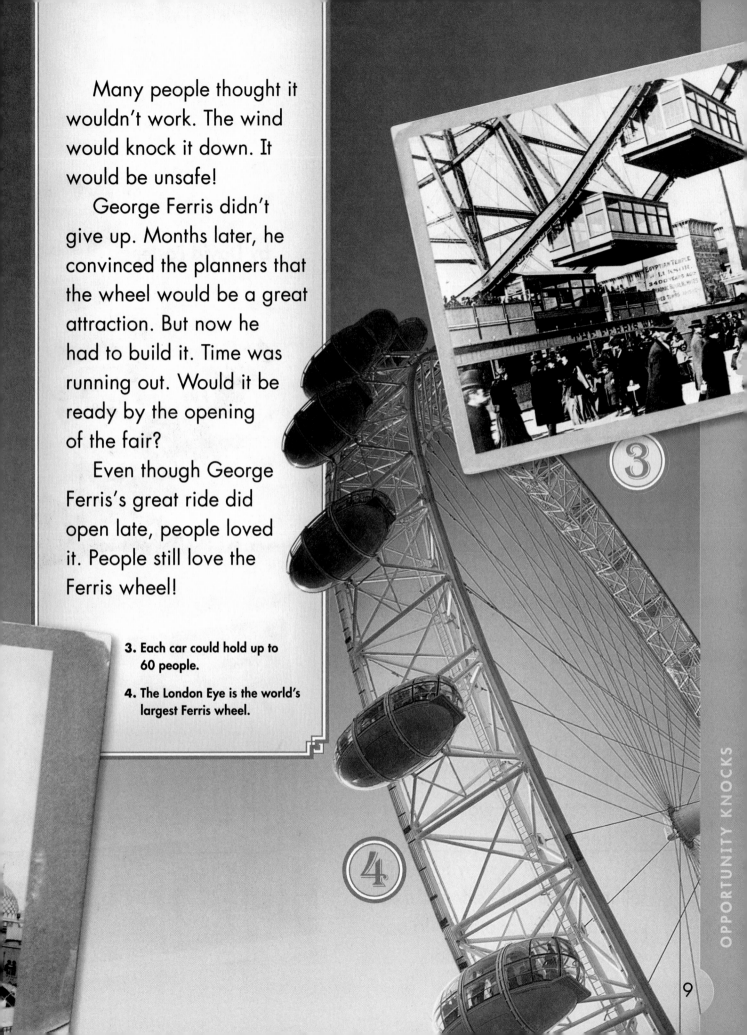

Many people thought it wouldn't work. The wind would knock it down. It would be unsafe!

George Ferris didn't give up. Months later, he convinced the planners that the wheel would be a great attraction. But now he had to build it. Time was running out. Would it be ready by the opening of the fair?

Even though George Ferris's great ride did open late, people loved it. People still love the Ferris wheel!

3. Each car could hold up to 60 people.

4. The London Eye is the world's largest Ferris wheel.

THEY DIDN'T GIVE UP

by David Foster

In 1936, Ted Geisel was on a ship from the United States to Europe. On the long journey, he listened to the steady rhythm of the ship's engine. As days passed, Ted wrote a children's story that had the same rhythm.

His conviction was that children would love the story. But Ted had to find a way to print and sell it. Ted sent the story to one publisher after another. No one wanted to publish his story.

Can you imagine the sound of this ship's engine?

Some people suggested he give up. Ted didn't listen. He sent his story to more than forty publishers. Finally, someone said yes! They would publish his story.

Children loved his book—a lot. They still do. In fact, you may have read this book too! It's called *And to Think That I Saw It on Mulberry Street.* Since then, Ted Geisel wrote many other stories. Most people know him as Dr. Seuss.

Dr. Seuss wrote and illustrated 44 children's books.

One of Joanne's favorite subjects in school was English.

A WORLD OF WIZARDS

Circumstances were not very good for a young mother and her small daughter. They were living in a cold apartment in Scotland.

The mother's name was Joanne, and she wanted to be a writer. In her apartment and a neighborhood cafe, she wrote as often as she could. In between writing and caring for her daughter, Joanne worked as a teacher.

She was motivated by her conviction that she had a great story to tell.

If her book were successful, it would mean a better life for her and her daughter. So Joanne never gave up.

Finally, in 1996, she finished her story. It then took over a year to publish her book. When it was published, the book was an instant hit with children of all ages. It was called *Harry Potter and the Sorcerer's Stone*. Joanne is J.K. Rowling. This was the first book of many about her famous character Harry Potter.

J.K. Rowling took the opportunity to write a series of popular books.

J.K. Rowling's books have been made into popular movies.

John wanted a magazine that showed all the great things African Americans were doing.

MOTIVATED TO SUCCEED

In the early 1900s, there were not many opportunities for African Americans. Many families believed that they would improve their circumstances by moving to the North. There were more jobs, and their children would receive a better education.

John H. Johnson's family moved from Arkansas to Chicago in the 1930s. John became an excellent student. He attended two of Chicago's best universities before pursuing his dream. He wanted to start a magazine for African Americans.

John H. Johnson's refusal to accept failure led to his great success.

John needed money to start his magazine. But back then, banks didn't want to lend money to African Americans. They thought that African Americans wouldn't want to read this type of magazine.

The word "no" motivated John. It made him work harder. Finally, John was able to raise enough money.

In 1942, John printed the first copy of his magazine. It was a huge success. Today, *Ebony*, one of John H. Johnson's most famous magazines, is the number-one-selling magazine for African Americans.

As a soldier in World War I, Walt drove an ambulance.

THE WONDERFUL WORLD OF CARTOONS

In 1918, the United States was fighting in World War I. A young boy named Walt volunteered to join the Army, but he was rejected. He was just 16 years old.

Then someone suggested he join the Red Cross. Walt drove an ambulance during the war. He drew cartoon characters all over the ambulance.

After the war, Walt worked as an artist in his own company. He wanted to make movies. At the time, not many people were making cartoon movies.

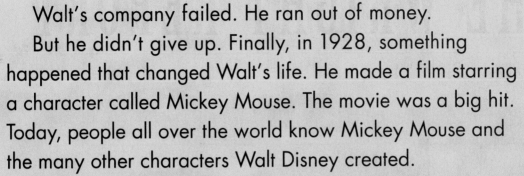

Walt's company failed. He ran out of money.

But he didn't give up. Finally, in 1928, something happened that changed Walt's life. He made a film starring a character called Mickey Mouse. The movie was a big hit. Today, people all over the world know Mickey Mouse and the many other characters Walt Disney created.

Do you have any great ideas? Remember these stories. At first you may fail, but don't ever give up!

Walt Disney's characters still bring joy to people's lives.

WHAT DO YOU THINK?

Choose one person that you read about. Tell what steps the person took to become a success.

THE WRIGHT REPORT

BY CHRISTINA RODRIGUEZ ~ ILLUSTRATED BY TERRY WIDENER

David heard his mom calling him. He pulled the covers over his head, thinking about his dream. He'd been taking his plane into a loop-the-loop. His mom called again, and David groaned.

At breakfast, David's parents talked to him about their meeting with his teacher. She said David procrastinates. He hadn't been finishing his work.

"Mrs. Sanger says you do good work when you try," his mom said. "We know that because of all the model planes you've built."

What difference does it make? David thought. *Math problems and book reports won't change my life. Now if I had a class about airplanes . . .*

"Well?" his dad asked. "Will you try to do better?"

"Yes," David mumbled.

At school, Mrs. Sanger announced, "Class, we're going to the library. I want you to find a book about a famous person or event in history. You will read this book and then write a book report about it."

David walked around the library randomly looking at books. *Who cares what people did a long time ago?* he thought.

He looked at books with pictures of important people. They all looked so serious. No wonder he wasn't motivated.

The students needed to choose whom they were going to write about by the end of library period. David was still looking when Mrs. Sanger walked by him.

"David, don't procrastinate," she said. "Think about what *you* like!"

David shrugged. In one book a man with a beard was speaking into a tube—*boring*. A woman in a white dress was in a parade—*boring*. Two men were standing in front of an airplane—*hold on now*!

The airplane was an early glider. The men didn't look very old, but their clothes were old-fashioned.

"Mrs. Sanger, are these important people? I mean, important enough for a book report?"

"David, they're Orville and Wilbur Wright," she said.

21

"You love airplanes," Mrs. Sanger said. "This is a good opportunity to learn about how daring these men were."

David read on the bus. When the brothers were boys, their father gave them a flying toy powered by a rubber band. A man in France had devised the toy flying machine. The brothers dreamt of building things.

David didn't think anyone could love flying as much as he did. He had a lot in common with the Wright brothers!

The brothers' simple toy sparked a big dream. As the Wright brothers got older, they came up with some amazing ideas.

First, they studied how birds flew. Then they devised different flying machines. Finally, they invented an airplane. Kitty Hawk, North Carolina, would be the perfect spot to test it.

When David arrived home, his mom asked, "Do you want a snack before starting your homework?"

"Can I take it to my room?" he asked.

David kept reading. He didn't feel like he was doing schoolwork. He was excited. *I wish I could have met those guys,* he thought. *People told them they would never make their dream happen, but they kept trying.*

After dinner, Dad came into his room.

"Still reading?" he asked.

"No, Dad. I'm writing," said David. "Want to read it?"

Dad read the report. "The Wright brothers remind me of you," Dad said. "Maybe someday you'll make airplane history."

In class, David was the first one to read his report. He brought model airplanes along to show the class. It was easy.

"I wish we could do projects like this all of the time," David told Mrs. Sanger later.

David had never realized that there were so many books about flying and airplanes in the library. He had a lot of reading to do!

WHAT DO YOU THINK?

How do David's feelings about book reports change from the beginning of the story to the end?

74th Street

by Myra Cohn Livingston

Hey, this little kid gets roller skates.
She puts them on.
She stands up and almost
flops over backwards.
She sticks out a foot like
she's going somewhere and
falls down and
smacks her hand. She
grabs hold of a step to get up and
sticks out the other foot and
slides about six inches and
falls and
skins her knee.

And then, you know what?

She brushes off the dirt and the
blood and puts some
spit on it and then
sticks out the other foot

again.

Ladder to the Sky

by Sheree Fitch

Do you know
If you try
You really can
Touch the sky?

Lean a ladder
Against the moon
And climb, climb high
Talk to the stars
And leave your handprints
All across the sky

Jump on a cloud
And spend the day
Trampoline-jumping
Through the air
Climb a rainbow
And watch the world
From way up there
Then ride the rainbow slide
Back home.

4 YOU 2 DO

Word Play

Unscramble these words. Then use the correct word in each sentence.

desevdi   **tancrumiccses**   **demlo**

You are a _____ student. You always do your homework.

The _____ of his life made his success seem greater.

You _____ a great plan for making the plane.

Making Connections

The Wright brothers motivated David to do well. Choose one person you read about. How might he or she motivate someone?

On Paper

Think about a friend who wants to achieve a difficult goal such as learning to play a musical instrument. Write sentences that give advice. Motivate your friend to succeed!

Answers for Word Play: model, circumstances, devised

Challenges

Contents

Challenges

CIVIL RIGHTS

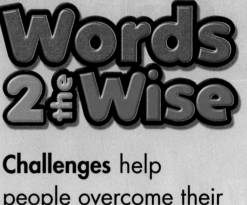

Words 2 the Wise

Challenges help people overcome their fears and achieve great things. As you read, think about how you can challenge yourself to achieve greatness.

33

The Secret of Success

Have you ever faced a big task or challenge? Thomas Edison, one of the world's greatest inventors, faced thousands of challenges. But he knew that the secret to his success was perseverance.

Thomas Edison was born in Milan, Ohio, in 1847. As a young boy, Edison became interested in science. This led him to become an inventor.

Thomas Edison and his phonograph invention

"Genius is one percent inspiration and ninety-nine percent perspiration."

–Thomas A. Edison

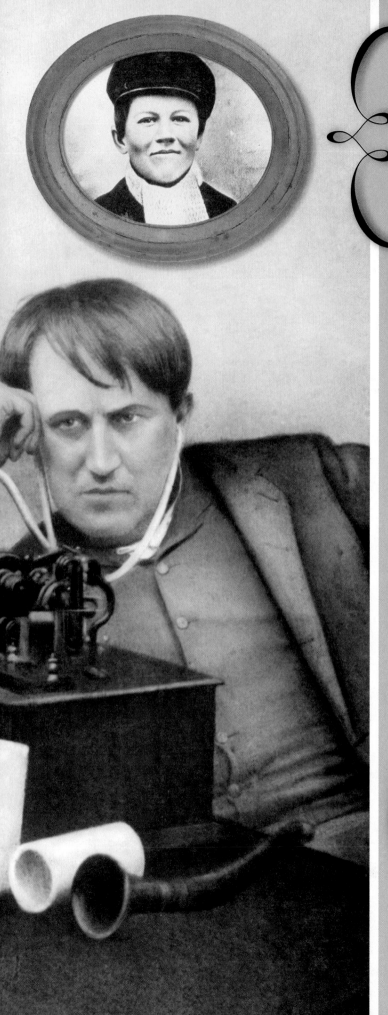

"If I find 10,000 ways something won't work, I haven't failed. I am not discouraged, because every wrong attempt discarded is often a step forward . . ."

–Thomas A. Edison

In 1868, Thomas Edison invented a machine that counted votes at elections. At the time, no one wanted to buy it. Edison did not give up. He kept working on more of his ideas.

Edison's printing telegraph was a little like text messaging.

Edison was an example of what hard work can accomplish. From his laboratory in Menlo Park, New Jersey, he conducted thousands of experiments. Many of them failed. Some of them you might use today.

In 1877, he made one of his greatest inventions. He invented the phonograph. This invention allowed people to listen to music in their own homes.

The movie camera was one of Edison's many inventions.

"The three things that are most essential to achievement are common sense, hard work, and stick-to-it-ive-ness . . ."

—Thomas A. Edison

"If we all did the things we are really capable of doing, we would literally astound ourselves . . ."

—Thomas A. Edison

Edison faced many obstacles before he achieved success. He even faced difficulties as a student. But he overcame those hurdles and became a successful inventor.

If you work hard and persevere, you might just surprise yourself about what you can achieve.

Edison didn't invent the light bulb, but he made it better.

Hurdles to Success

by Alef Lett

What do a pilot, a brain surgeon, and a civil rights leader have in common? Each of them had hurdles to overcome before becoming successful.

Ben Carson, 1969

A Tough Decision

Ben Carson felt that he was not as smart as the other kids in his school. He had a difficult time. Sometimes he got into trouble at school.

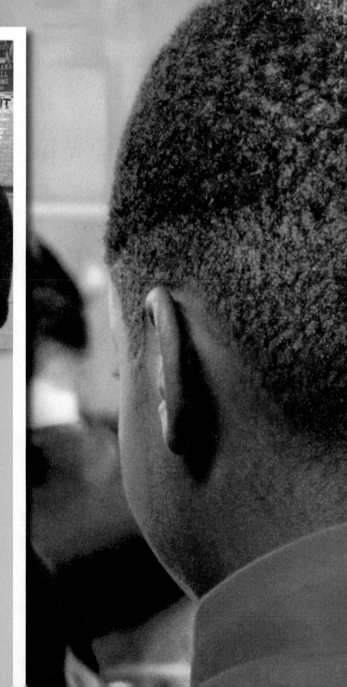

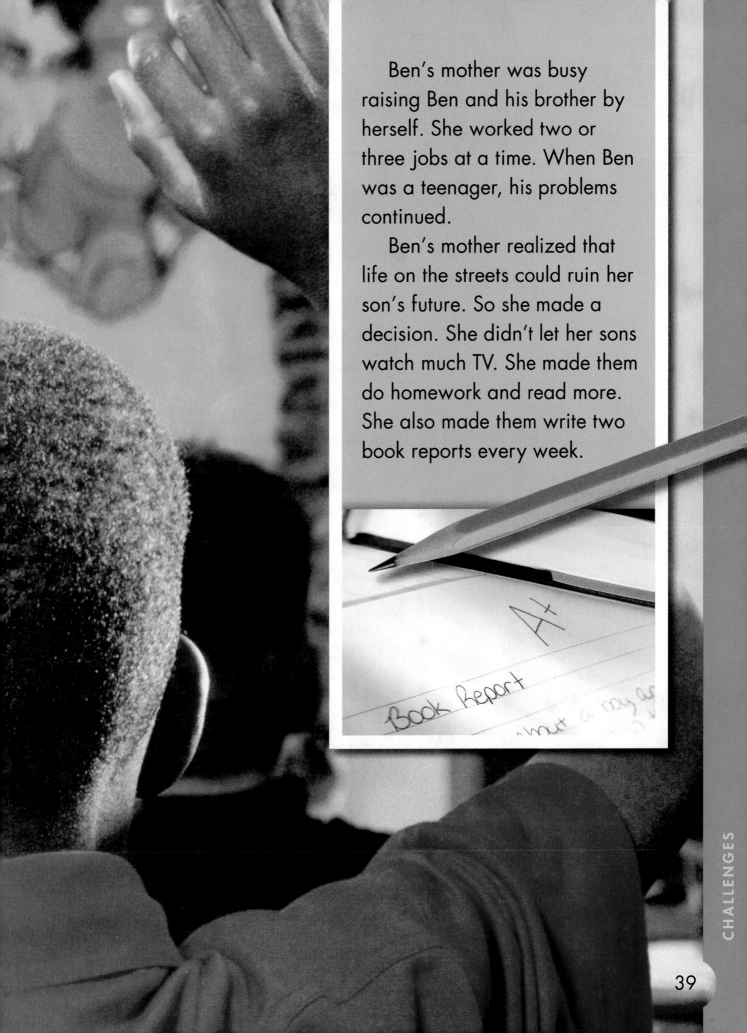

Ben's mother was busy raising Ben and his brother by herself. She worked two or three jobs at a time. When Ben was a teenager, his problems continued.

Ben's mother realized that life on the streets could ruin her son's future. So she made a decision. She didn't let her sons watch much TV. She made them do homework and read more. She also made them write two book reports every week.

A⁺

Book Report

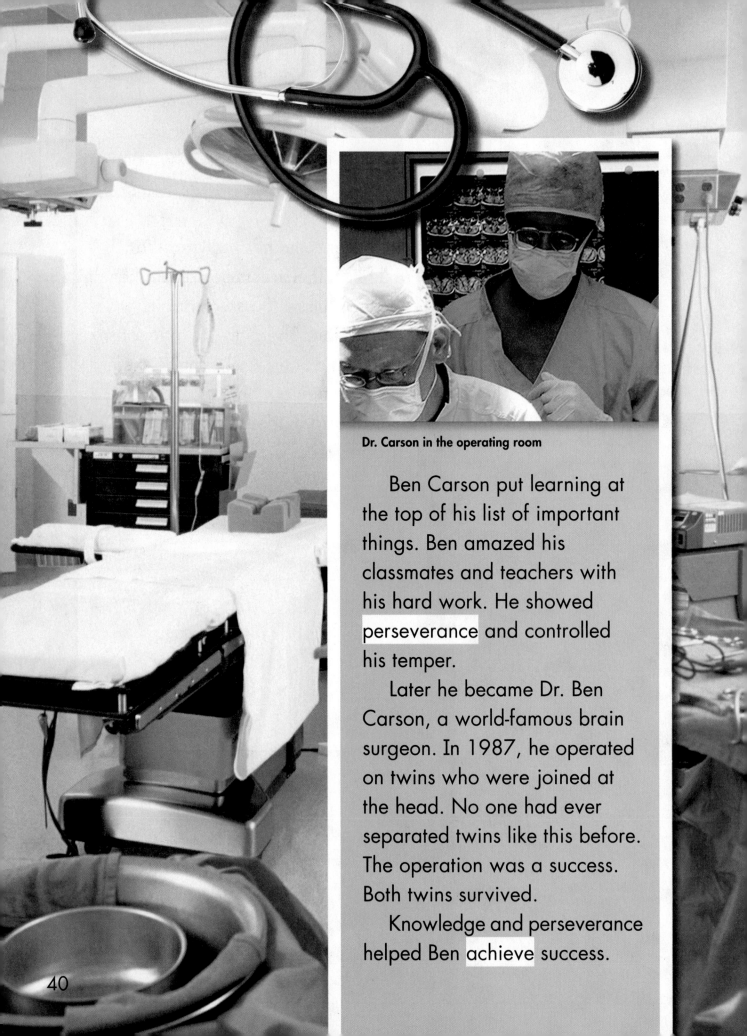

Dr. Carson in the operating room

Ben Carson put learning at the top of his list of important things. Ben amazed his classmates and teachers with his hard work. He showed perseverance and controlled his temper.

Later he became Dr. Ben Carson, a world-famous brain surgeon. In 1987, he operated on twins who were joined at the head. No one had ever separated twins like this before. The operation was a success. Both twins survived.

Knowledge and perseverance helped Ben achieve success.

Ann Baumgartner Carl

She Did It!

Ann Baumgartner Carl had her own hurdles to get over. As a child, she was shy and not very confident.

Ann's uncle had a ranch in Colorado. Once when she was working there, she had to bring the milk cows in. A storm was coming. She was scared, but she went to the pasture anyway and did her job. This helped her be more confident in her life.

WASPs during World War II

Ann Carl always wanted to fly planes. At the time, people thought that only men should fly. So Ann joined the Air Force. She and other women flew planes from factories to air bases. They were called Women Airforce Service Pilots, or WASPs.

Still, Ann wanted to test new jets. She knew she could do it. Finally, the Air Force chose Ann. She was the first woman to test jets. Ann achieved her dream of being a test pilot.

Ann flew a Curtis A-25 like this one.

Dolores Huerta

The Right Moves

Dolores Huerta (h-WEAR-ta) was born in California. She was raised around farm workers. Many farm workers were migrants. They came for the harvest. Then they traveled on to other farms or returned home. The work was hard, and the pay was low.

Dolores Huerta's mother ran a small hotel and restaurant. Sometimes she let migrant farm workers stay for free.

Dolores Huerta spoke out for the rights of workers.

Later Dolores became a teacher. Many of her students were children of migrant workers. The students were often hungry. They needed clothes and books too. Dolores decided to stop teaching. She put her efforts into organizing migrant workers.

Dolores Huerta began to teach the workers about their rights. She worked with Cesar Chavez (SAY-zar CHA-vez), another civil rights leader. They began an organization that helped migrant workers get better pay, better places to live, and better health care.

CIVIL RIGHTS

Dolores Huerta led marches to help win rights for migrant workers. She has been honored for her work by universities and presidents.

Dolores Huerta had to overcome many hurdles. Some people didn't want the farm workers to have rights. Sometimes these groups used violence against the farm workers. Dolores organized peaceful meetings and protests. After years of perseverance, Dolores helped to improve the lives of migrant workers.

These three people jumped over hurdles to achieve their dreams. The world is a better place because they did.

What Do You Think?

How did Ben, Ann, and Dolores persevere?

SAMMY THE SOFA

by Douglass Francis   illustrated by Jim Steck

Hi, I'm Ronnie. I want to tell you a story about my brother Sammy. He's in fourth grade. I know fourth grade is hard. But Sammy is timid, so it's harder for him.

When he turned six, Mom and Dad invited kids over for a party. The kids came, but Sammy wasn't there. Well, he was there. He just wouldn't come out from behind the sofa.

It was crazy singing "Happy Birthday" to a sofa.

After that, Sammy spent a lot of time behind the sofa. Sammy kept a pillow, a flashlight, a few books, and some games back there. He would peek out to watch TV. Sammy was timid, but he wasn't always quiet. At times, Sammy would yell out things from behind the sofa. Once, Aunt Betty almost fainted when Sammy yelled "Touchdown!" during a football game on TV. She had forgotten he was back there.

Sammy has two loyal friends, Scott and Josh. He would come out from behind the sofa to play games with them. And Sammy also comes out to go to school.

Some older kids at school call him "Sammy the Sofa." He hates that nickname. And I get furious when people pick on him!

As long as my brother is shy, people will never know his real personality. He is really funny, a great singer, and a football trivia whiz!

Last month, my best friend Monica and I were watching TV at my house. Sammy was behind the sofa.

We were watching a talent show and someone was singing. Suddenly, a voice was singing along. It was Sammy.

Monica's mouth dropped open. "What a great voice!" she said.

Sammy shut up when he heard that. But Monica didn't. "Sammy," she said to the sofa, "next Thursday, we're having tryouts for the school play. You're going to try out."

"I can't," Sammy cracked. "I have to dust and flip my sofa pillows that day."

Monica looked at me, and we knew what to do. We lifted the sofa and carried it across the room and blocked the door. Sammy was out in the open with nowhere to go. He was furious!

"Sammy, you would be great in the play. The story fits your personality," she said. That's Monica! She's got perseverance.

Monica went on. "The play's kind of silly. It is about things in a house coming to life at night."

Sammy was quiet. He was thinking. "What kinds of things?" he asked curiously.

"Oh, dishes and furniture," said Monica.

It sounded strange, but Sammy's eyes lit up. "Furniture?" he asked. "Like a singing sofa?" His voice sounded clear and confident.

"Well, it's a singing chair right now. But it could be a sofa," said Monica.

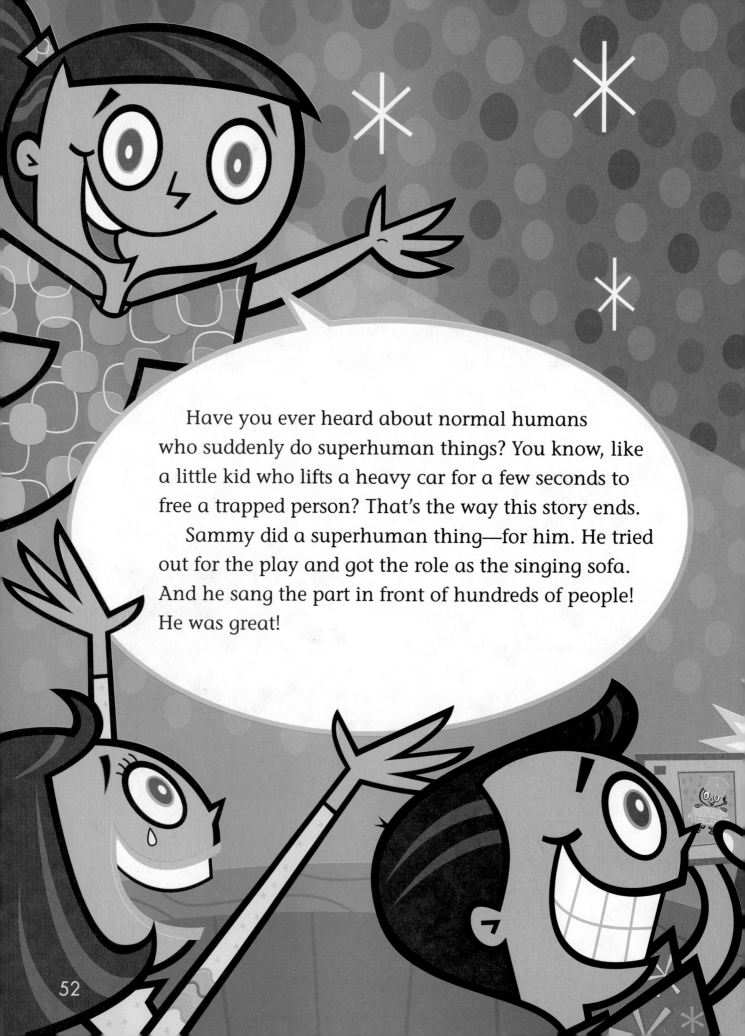

Have you ever heard about normal humans who suddenly do superhuman things? You know, like a little kid who lifts a heavy car for a few seconds to free a trapped person? That's the way this story ends.

Sammy did a superhuman thing—for him. He tried out for the play and got the role as the singing sofa. And he sang the part in front of hundreds of people! He was great!

My timid brother found enough confidence to do this. It was a big hurdle to jump, but he did it!

Sammy's shyness problems are not over. They may last a while, even into fifth grade. But I know that one day Sammy the Singing Sofa will be Sammy the Star.

In the meantime, if you want a signed picture of Sammy the Singing Sofa, let me know. I'll see what I can do.

WHAT DO YOU THINK?

Why do you think Sammy decided to try out for the play?

Climbing to the

In 1852, Radhanath Sickdhar (RAHD-ha-nahth sick-DAHR) worked for four years to measure the height of a mountain in Nepal. This mountain was then called Peak XV.* Now his hard work and perseverance would pay off. He calculated that the mountain was 29,002 feet high.

Peak XV, or Mount Everest, is the tallest mountain in the world. It has been the dream of many to reach its top. This is a challenging dream to accomplish.

*XV are Roman numerals for the number 15.

The view from the top of Mount Everest is incredible.

Top of the World

The height of Mount Everest has drawn many climbers to scale it. Thousands of people have climbed Mount Everest. What kinds of abilities do climbers need? Perseverance, physical fitness, and common sense are necessary to reach the top safely. Today, climbers carry oxygen tanks. They wear layers of light clothing that keep them warm on the cold, high mountain. People will continue to try to climb Everest as long as the mountain stands.

Below, Left to Right: Tenzing Norgay and Edmund Hillary were the first climbers to make it to the top in 1953; Erik Weihenmayer was the first blind person to climb Everest; in 1975, Junko Tabei was the first woman to reach the top; Yuichiro Miura climbed Everest when he was 70 years old.

4 You 2 Do

Word Play

A synonym is a word that means the same or nearly the same as another word. Find two synonyms in List B for each vocabulary word in List A.

A

hurdle
achieve
perseverance

B

finish   persistence
obstacle   barrier
accomplish   determination

Making Connections

What made Sammy decide to sing? What makes people forget about the hurdles and do something they really want to do?

On Paper

Write about a goal you have for yourself. What steps can you take to reach this goal?

Answers for Word Play: hurdle: obstacle, barrier; achieve: finish, accomplish; perseverance: persistence, determination.

56

American

Journeys

Contents

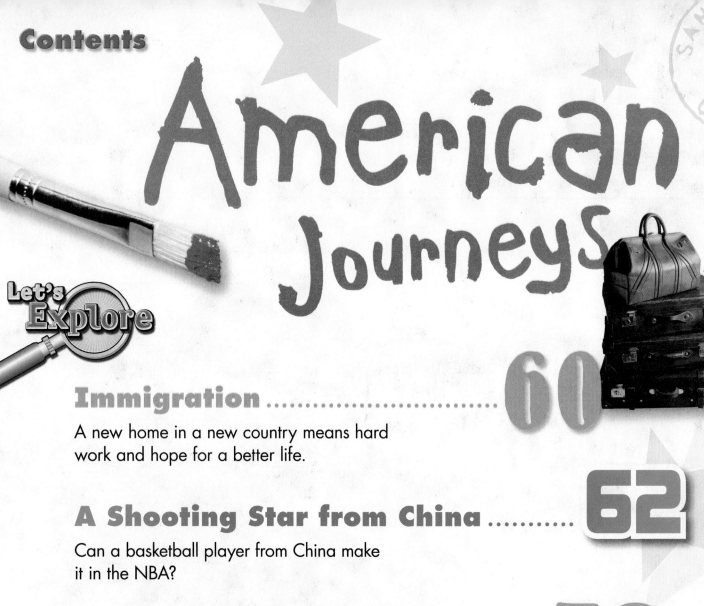

American Journeys

Let's Explore

58

Words 2 the Wise

People from all over the world make **American journeys.** Many of these people share the same experiences once they get here. As you read, think about what it might be like to leave your home country to live in another country.

Let's Explore

Immigration

Have you ever had to move to a different city or state? Was it difficult? Some people move to the United States from different countries. We call these people immigrants.

Up until 1930, most immigrants came to the United States from Europe. Immigrants sailed across the Atlantic Ocean on ships. Some ships docked at Ellis Island in New York.

Immigrants came here for many reasons.
For some Europeans it was difficult to find work.
For others their countries were at war. Still others
were looking for freedom. They all hoped for a
better life in the United States.

Today most immigrants come from Asia, Africa,
and Latin America. They come here for many of the
same reasons as earlier immigrants. They hope to
find new opportunities and to live in freedom.

Do you know someone from another country?
What opportunities did they hope to find?

A Shooting Star from China

by Rob Rainer

Today basketball stars are not just found on American courts. Basketball is an international game. Yao Ming (YOW MING) brought his talent for basketball to the United States from China. His teammates, friends, family, and fans think Yao is amazing. And not just because he is seven feet, six inches tall!

Yao Ming came to the United States to play professional basketball. He plays center for the Houston Rockets.

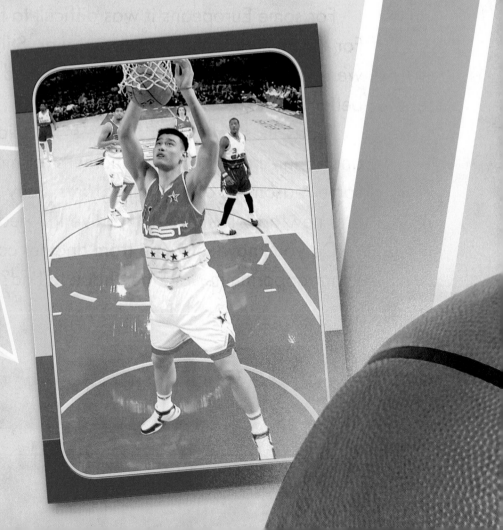

Yao has become one of the best players in the NBA.

Yao Ming spent his childhood in Shanghai, China's largest city.

Yao Ming was born in China in 1980. Both of Yao Ming's parents are over six feet tall. They played professional basketball in China in the 1970s.

Yao was always tall for his age. In kindergarten, he was so tall that he had to buy an adult ticket to ride the bus. When Yao was 13 years old, he was six-and-a-half feet tall. Every year he kept getting taller and taller.

Yao went to a school that let him practice basketball many hours each day. As he grew taller, his basketball skills improved.

At age 19, Yao began to play for the Chinese national team. He quickly became the best player in China. People in China loved watching him play. But Yao dreamed of playing in the United States. In 2002, Yao's dream came true. The Houston Rockets picked Yao to play for them.

Yao's parents are very proud of him.

Yao Ming and his parents said good-bye to China. They boarded a plane that would take them to their new home in the United States.

But immigration for Yao was different from the immigration experience that most people have when they come to the United States. Yao was picked up at the airport. He was offered a job that would pay him millions of dollars. Still there were challenges that he had to face.

One Name, Two Countries

Americans know this basketball superstar as *Yao Ming*. But if Yao grew up in America, he would be called *Ming Yao*. Ming is really his first name. In China, the family name is said first.

PASSPORT

PASS

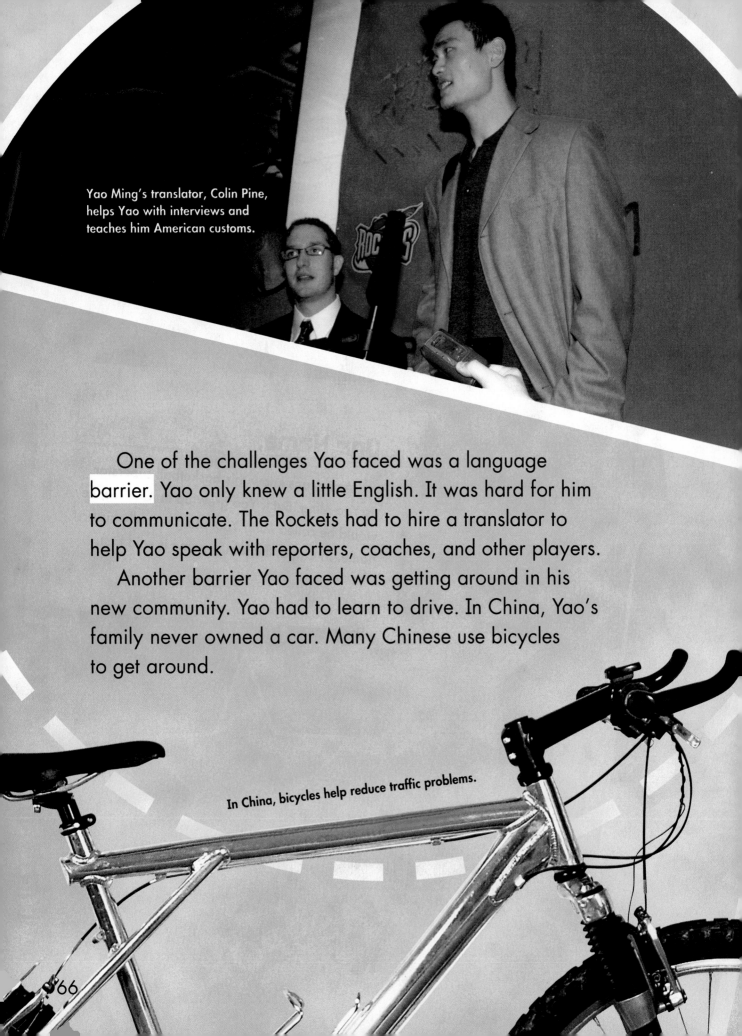

Yao Ming's translator, Colin Pine, helps Yao with interviews and teaches him American customs.

One of the challenges Yao faced was a language barrier. Yao only knew a little English. It was hard for him to communicate. The Rockets had to hire a translator to help Yao speak with reporters, coaches, and other players.

Another barrier Yao faced was getting around in his new community. Yao had to learn to drive. In China, Yao's family never owned a car. Many Chinese use bicycles to get around.

In China, bicycles help reduce traffic problems.

Eventually Yao had to take a driving test. One teammate said Yao was more nervous for this test than he was for playing basketball.

Yao had many challenges on the basketball court too. The NBA style of play is different from the Chinese style. Yao had to learn to communicate with his teammates. On the court players communicate not just with words, but also with moves and gestures. At first Yao appeared out of place. It was a difficult adjustment.

Yao had to learn fast in the NBA.

Yao Ming is very popular
with American fans.

Soon Yao did adjust to the NBA style of play. Today American and Chinese fans are thrilled. Yao can slam-dunk. He can also shoot amazing three-point baskets.

Living in the spotlight was another challenge for Yao. He is shy. As an international superstar, fans were always asking for his autograph. Shoe companies wanted Yao in their commercials. Slowly he began to enjoy the support from fans. Yao sometimes communicates with his fans over his Internet site.

Yao shares his journal
entries on his Web site.

Yao Ming carried the torch during the Olympics.

Yao Ming spends most of the year living in the United States. But he is still a Chinese citizen. He even plays on the Chinese national basketball team for part of the year. He represented China in the 2000 and 2004 Olympics. Yao feels his success is China's success too.

At one time it was impossible for a Chinese citizen to play basketball in the United States. Yao proved that "with time, anything is possible."

What Do You Think?

Why did Yao work so hard to improve his English?

Becoming an American

by Mary Clare Goller

Albert moved from Germany to New York in 1907. Elena moved from Brazil to Chicago in 2007.

New York, September 2, 1907

Our family is in America now. My father carried his carpentry tools along on the ship. He hopes to start working soon.

I walked by my new school today. The building looks very different from my school in Germany. I wonder if other children will speak German. I know only a few words in English! Mother and Father are trying to learn English too. Father wants to make chairs. He needs customers!

Chicago, September 2, 2007

My family flew to America from Brazil. Now we are living in Chicago, Illinois. I couldn't read many of the signs at the airport. Everything is in English. I don't smell the ocean anymore. Here tall buildings hide the sun.

The school my sisters and I will go to is around the corner from our house. My mother and father can take the train to work. They are both university professors.

New York, October 2, 1907

I am not the only student who doesn't know English well. Others are from Germany too. I try to say "good day" to my teacher instead of guten Tag (GOO-ten tahg). But I feel awkward trying to speak with the American kids. I carefully copy what the teacher writes on the blackboard.

Father has built a new chair for a customer. He carved beautiful designs on it. The chair is like the ones he built in Germany.

Chicago, October 2, 2007

The great oak trees are changing colors. I miss the sunny days in Brazil, but I appreciate the colors of fall here. Fall colors remind me of Brazil.

Today my sisters and I tried on winter clothes. I am not used to being covered up like a bear! My parents have good occupations, but I want a different one. I want to design new styles of clothes for this cold climate.

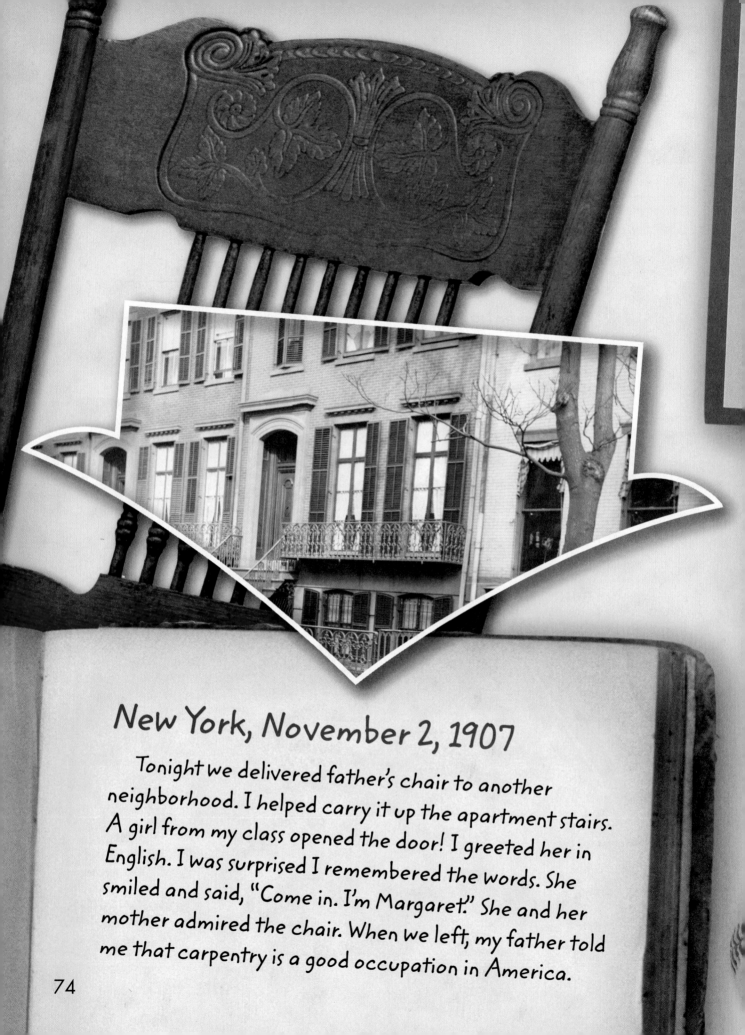

New York, November 2, 1907

Tonight we delivered father's chair to another neighborhood. I helped carry it up the apartment stairs. A girl from my class opened the door! I greeted her in English. I was surprised I remembered the words. She smiled and said, "Come in. I'm Margaret." She and her mother admired the chair. When we left, my father told me that carpentry is a good occupation in America.

Chicago, November 2, 2007

At recess we can play any sport we want. I like "four-square." The gym has so much equipment. I'm not used to so many basketballs, kick balls, jump ropes, and baseballs.

After school, I raced my sisters to our house. We saw our neighbor, Mr. Foster. He walks with a cane and calls us the "Princesses from Brazil!" I don't feel awkward talking with him in English. He is kind and teaches us new words.

New York, December 2, 1907

More customers want to buy father's hand-carved chairs. Our village in Germany is tiny compared to New York! I appreciate this busy city. We can become well-known carpenters!

I want to help father carve the wood and make chairs too. But he says I must stay in school. When I finish, we can go into business together. Father plans to open a shop soon. I can help him talk to the customers in English.

Chicago, December 2, 2007

We had the first winter snow! Big plows cleared the snow away! Buses kept running too. In some places in Brazil, the roads would wash out after a rainstorm. Sometimes there was no electricity for days. Here, the lights stay on, and workers clear the streets.

Mr. Foster needed to clear the sidewalk in front of his house. My sisters and I gladly helped. Then the neighborhood kids helped us build our first snowman!

What Do You Think?

What do you think Albert likes best about living in the United States? What do you think Elena likes best?

Traditional Clothing

Clothing is a part of every culture. It tells a lot about us.

Japanese Kimono

Japanese and Japanese Americans wear *kimonos* and *happi* coats to celebrate their culture. To wear a kimono, you need to wear a few different pieces of clothing. The kimono pieces are made of silk. The *obi* is a belt that wraps around a person's waist. A sash, called an *obijime* (oh-bee-jee-me) helps keep the obi in place. It can take almost two hours to get dressed in a kimono!

West African Dashiki

In hot Nigerian weather and in the United States, men and boys wear colorful *dashikis* (da-SHEE-kees) to show their heritage. The dashiki is a loose-fitting tunic, or shirt. The tunic is made from colorful fabric. Sometimes the fabric is dyed by hand. The tunics cover pants of similar fabric.

Indian Sari

The sari (SAH-ree) is the oldest known traditional dress in the world. For about 5,000 years, Indian women have been draping the colorful cloth around themselves. The sari is made from almost 20 feet of fabric. Women look graceful when the fabric is wrapped around the body. Another loose piece of fabric usually hangs over the shoulder.

Greek Foustanela

Boys celebrate their Greek heritage when they wear a *foustanela* (fohs-TAN-el-la). This traditional outfit is named for the pleated white skirt, or foustanela. Today, Greek soldiers still wear foustanelas.

A white shirt, a woolen vest, a sash worn around the waist, and shoes with large pompoms are all part of the outfit.

4 You 2 Do

Word Play

This week you read about immigration. See if you can unscramble the letters below to find some of this week's vocabulary words.

1. riebrar
2. kawdraw
3. copactusoni
4. tigramimion

Making Connections

How was Yao Ming's experience in a new country different from Albert and Elena's? What was one thing they all had in common?

On Paper

What part of your culture would you take with you if you were to move to a new country? What types of food and clothing represent your country?

Answers for Word Play: barrier, awkward, occupations, immigration

GRAND *Gestures*

Contents

GRAND Gestures

Words 2 the Wise

Have you ever helped someone by giving up something that was important to you? What a grand gesture! As you read, think about the **grand gestures** other people have made and why they made them.

85

Let's Explore Grand Gestures

Have you ever given a family member a card or a gift to show that you care? If so, you made a gesture. A gesture is something you do to show your feelings or intentions. Giving a gift is a nice gesture!

But what distinguishes a nice gesture from a grand gesture? You make a grand gesture when you give up something to help others.

Pretend you are saving to buy a new video game. In the meantime, your class is determined to raise money for a trip to the science museum. Everyone tries, but the class does not make much headway raising money. Progress is slow.

You decide to give up some of your savings so that others can go on the trip. Your gesture inspires others to do the same. This means that everyone can go to the museum. Now *that* is a grand gesture!

GRAND GESTURES

LIBRARY HERO

by Cornelius James • illustrated by Judy Love

Everyone in Salem, Massachusetts, was talking about the bad news. It was on television and the radio. The Salem school system was running out of money. Eighty teachers and other people who worked for the schools would lose their jobs! The school libraries would close!

How could this happen? Jonathan Marrero, age ten, could not stay quiet. He was determined to do something about this!

Jonathan thought about the money he had saved in a box. It was a large sum. *Would it help?* he wondered.

Jonathan wrote what a newspaper later referred to as "a beautiful note." He took the note and his money to his librarian at Saltonstall School. He wanted her to use the money to keep the library open.

The librarian was touched that Jonathan cared so much. But she could not keep his money. She thanked him and gave the money back. Still, this determined boy did not give up.

Jonathan had another idea. He asked his brother and several friends to help him collect money for the schools. For three days, they knocked on doors in Salem. In the rain and snow, they walked up and down the streets. Altogether, they collected $1,500!

Jonathan and his friends were making progress, but the schools needed more money. Jonathan had to apply himself even harder.

Jonathan thought of more efficient ways to earn money. He made hot chocolate and lollipops and sold them in front of his house. After a snowstorm, he shoveled many driveways and sidewalks.

In this way, Jonathan earned about $1,000 more. He was making headway toward his goal.

As more and more people in the community found out what Jonathan was doing, they wanted to help too. Children, adults, and even businesses gave money.

During three weeks of hard work, Jonathan raised more than $2,400. Even better, he brought people together. Other people saw what a ten-year-old boy was doing, and they were inspired to do something as well.

By giving up his time and savings, Jonathan made a big difference. In the end, he helped raise enough money to save 47 of the 80 jobs that were due to be cut. His school's library stayed open too!

The governor of Massachusetts praised Jonathan for his efforts to help the schools. Governor Patrick said, "I love that you stepped up." He gave Jonathan a small blue pin shaped like Massachusetts.

The director of the New York Public Libraries also heard about Jonathan and sent him a letter. The director said that books and libraries had always been important to him too. He said, "That librarian is very lucky to have a friend like you."

This wasn't the first time Jonathan had put others first. Once, his class planned a trip to Boston. Each student was asked to raise $55 by selling candy. Jonathan sold his share. Then he held a yard sale and raised $170 more. He gave the money to his class to help kids who hadn't been able to sell much candy.

After he helped save the library, a national group learned about Jonathan. It chose him as its "Amazing Kid" of the month. Jonathan had indeed distinguished himself as a library hero!

Why does Jonathan give up his time and savings to help others? He says, "Helping is always a good thing."

WHAT DO YOU THINK?
What was Jonathan's grand gesture?

A Simple Gift

by Susan Light

Dan West sighed as he handed out cups of milk to the hungry children. It was 1937, and there was little food in Spain. The country was at war. The Indiana farmer had come to help. But he was discouraged. He did not have enough milk for all the children. And their families had no way of getting milk for them. "These children don't need a cup," he said. "They need a cow."

Dan West wanted to give more than just milk. He wanted to give a whole cow!

West Gets to Work

West returned home, but he kept thinking about the hungry children. He was determined to help. West knew that one heifer (HEF-uhr), or female cow, could provide a family with plenty of milk. But how could he send a cow across the ocean? West got to work and created a group called Heifers for Relief. In 1944, the group sent its first cows to hungry families in Puerto Rico.

"Seagoing Cowboys" delivered the first shipment of seventeen cows.

The first shipments of animals were made by boat. Later shipments were made by train or plane.

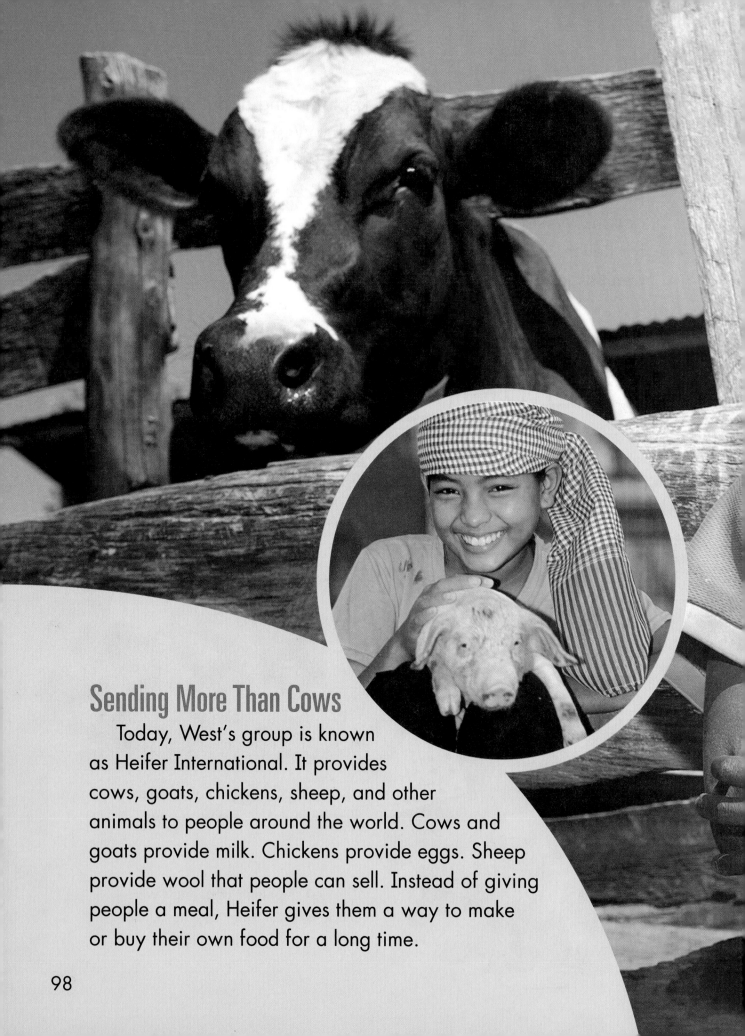

Sending More Than Cows

Today, West's group is known as Heifer International. It provides cows, goats, chickens, sheep, and other animals to people around the world. Cows and goats provide milk. Chickens provide eggs. Sheep provide wool that people can sell. Instead of giving people a meal, Heifer gives them a way to make or buy their own food for a long time.

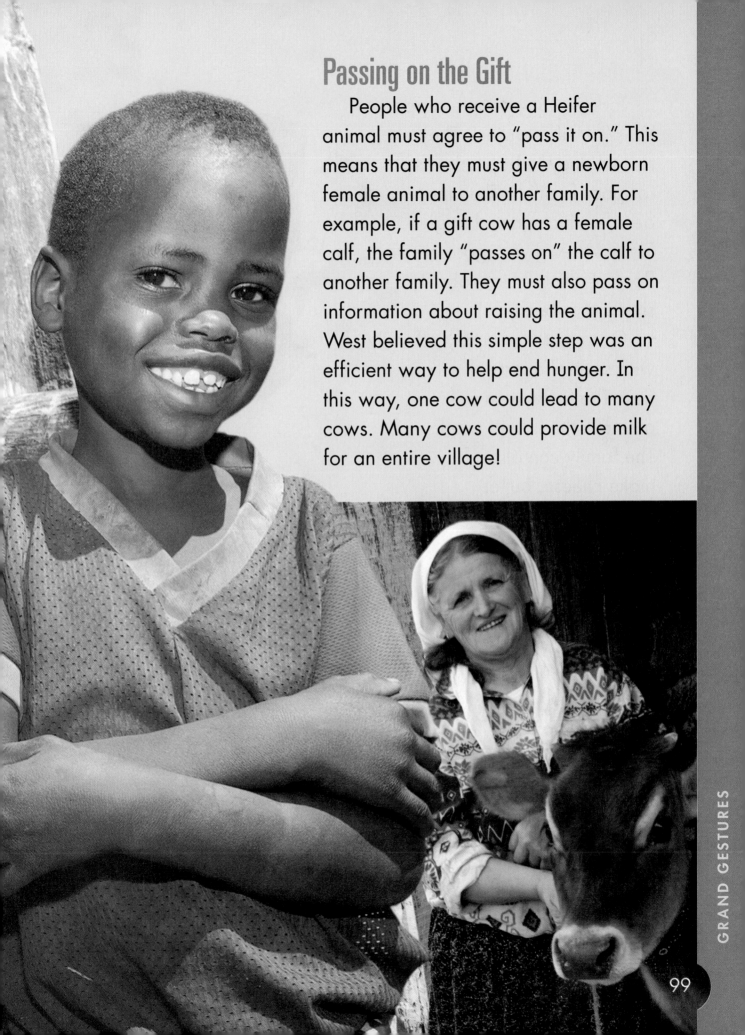

Passing on the Gift

People who receive a Heifer animal must agree to "pass it on." This means that they must give a newborn female animal to another family. For example, if a gift cow has a female calf, the family "passes on" the calf to another family. They must also pass on information about raising the animal. West believed this simple step was an efficient way to help end hunger. In this way, one cow could lead to many cows. Many cows could provide milk for an entire village!

Choosing an Animal

Today, many people support West's Heifer project. They raise money to buy animals for poor families. Then they decide which animal to give. Should they give a goat or a flock of chicks? How about a sheep or a bee hive?

One goat can supply a family with several quarts of milk a day. The family can sell any milk they don't need. The family can also make cheese, butter, or yogurt with the milk. They can eat or sell these products too.

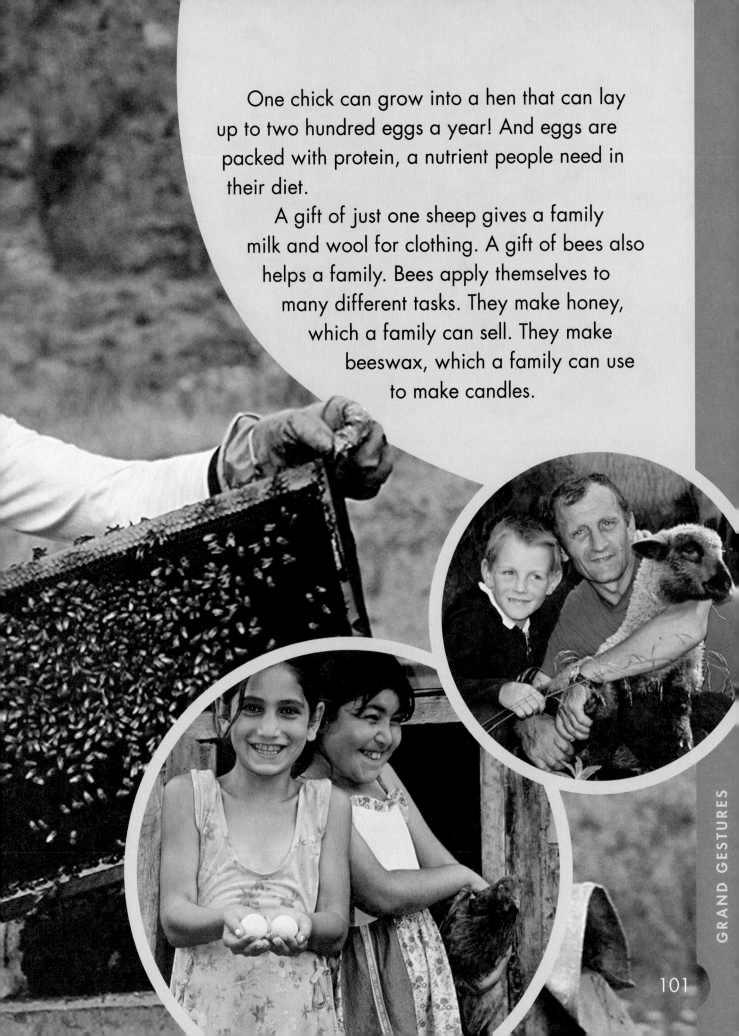

One chick can grow into a hen that can lay up to two hundred eggs a year! And eggs are packed with protein, a nutrient people need in their diet.

A gift of just one sheep gives a family milk and wool for clothing. A gift of bees also helps a family. Bees apply themselves to many different tasks. They make honey, which a family can sell. They make beeswax, which a family can use to make candles.

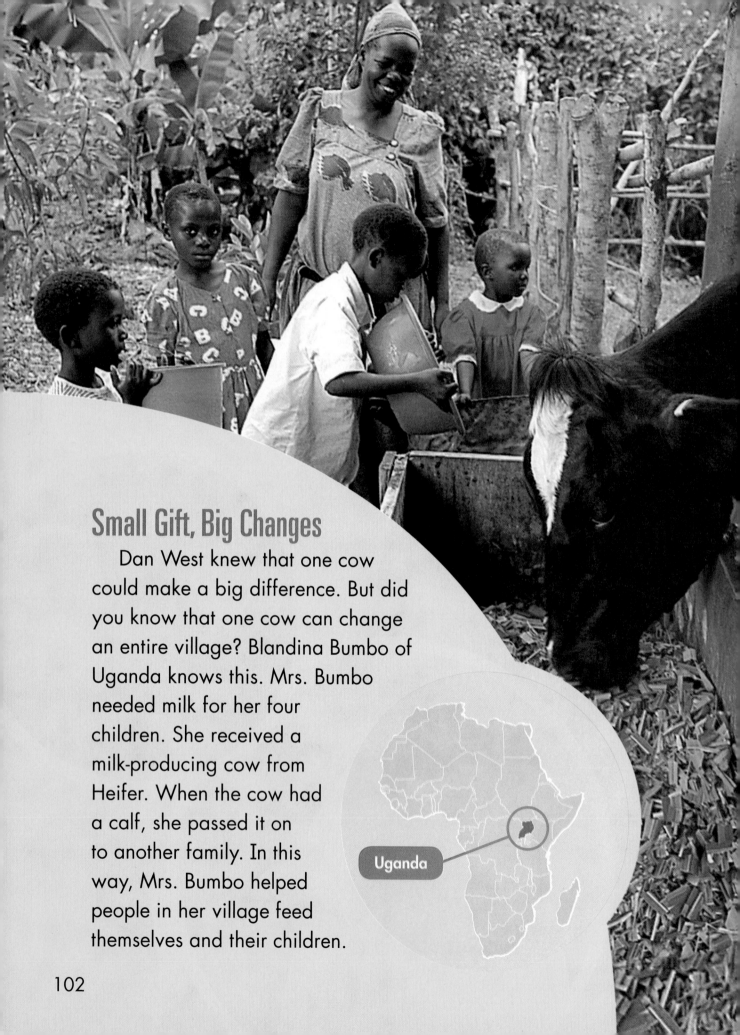

Small Gift, Big Changes

Dan West knew that one cow could make a big difference. But did you know that one cow can change an entire village? Blandina Bumbo of Uganda knows this. Mrs. Bumbo needed milk for her four children. She received a milk-producing cow from Heifer. When the cow had a calf, she passed it on to another family. In this way, Mrs. Bumbo helped people in her village feed themselves and their children.

Uganda

But Mrs. Bumbo thought the children's minds needed "food" too. The children needed a school. Then Mrs. Bumbo had an idea. She hired a teacher with the money she made selling milk. She set up a school in a nearby shed. Now, thirty children come to the school every day. They begin the day with a hot breakfast made with Mrs. Bumbo's milk. All it took was a big idea . . . and one small cow.

Heifer now has projects in over fifty countries, including the United States. Active projects are shown in green.

What Do You Think?

How does Heifer International help people make grand gestures?

A Birthday Give-Away

Have you ever thought about giving away your birthday gifts? Some children celebrate a birthday by giving away gifts—not keeping them. These special birthday parties are called give-away parties. Instead of presents, guests are asked to give money or other useful things. Then the birthday girl or boy gives the money or things to a group that helps others.

Some children have parties to help animals that are homeless.

Some children give their birthday present money to an animal shelter. The shelter uses it to care for dogs and cats that need homes. Other children help animals in shelters by asking their guests to bring pet supplies as gifts. The guests might bring dog food or kitty litter.

Still other children have parties to raise money for groups that fight a disease, such as cancer. Sometimes, big companies find out about these parties and give money too. Other times, they may give snacks for the party!

105

Some children have parties to collect clothing and toys for families who need them.

Some children give their birthday present money to a different group every year. One year, they might help a family whose home was damaged in a flood. The next year, they might buy something special for people in a nursing home.

Do kids have fun at these parties? You bet! They play games and get their faces painted. Everyone laughs a lot.

If you want to have a give-away party, talk it over with family members. They might know of groups that could use your help. Then check with the group you choose. See whether it needs money or something else. Send out invitations that request gifts for this group instead of gifts for you. Then have a great birthday!

You are invited to a birthday party!

Please bring gently used clothing instead of gifts.

I want to give the clothing to a homeless shelter.

Word Play

Make a word chain using the vocabulary words below. Begin by writing the word *headway*. Then use a letter in *headway* to write another vocabulary word. Continue in the same way with the rest of the words.

headway **apply** **efficient**
distinguish **determined**

Making Connections

How could Jonathan Marrero participate in Heifer International?

On Paper

Write about a grand gesture that you or someone you know has made. Explain why it was a grand gesture.

Space

Contents

Space

Let's Explore

Words 2 the Wise

Astronomers have found many new and exciting ways to explore **space.** When we learn about space, we also learn about Earth. As you read, think about what you know about space exploration.

Let's Explore

What's OUT There?

In the 1600s, scientists invented the telescope. Telescopes allow scientists to see distant planets, stars, and galaxies.

Galileo discovered four moons that orbit Jupiter.

Early Telescopes

Around 1608, a Dutch eyeglass maker began experimenting with lenses. He learned how to arrange the lenses to make objects that were far away look bigger. This is how the telescope was invented.

A famous scientist named Galileo (ga-li-LAY-o) improved the telescope. He built a telescope that made objects look 20 times bigger than they really were. Galileo turned his telescope towards the sky. He saw valleys and mountains on the surface of the moon.

This picture of stars was taken with the Spitzer telescope.

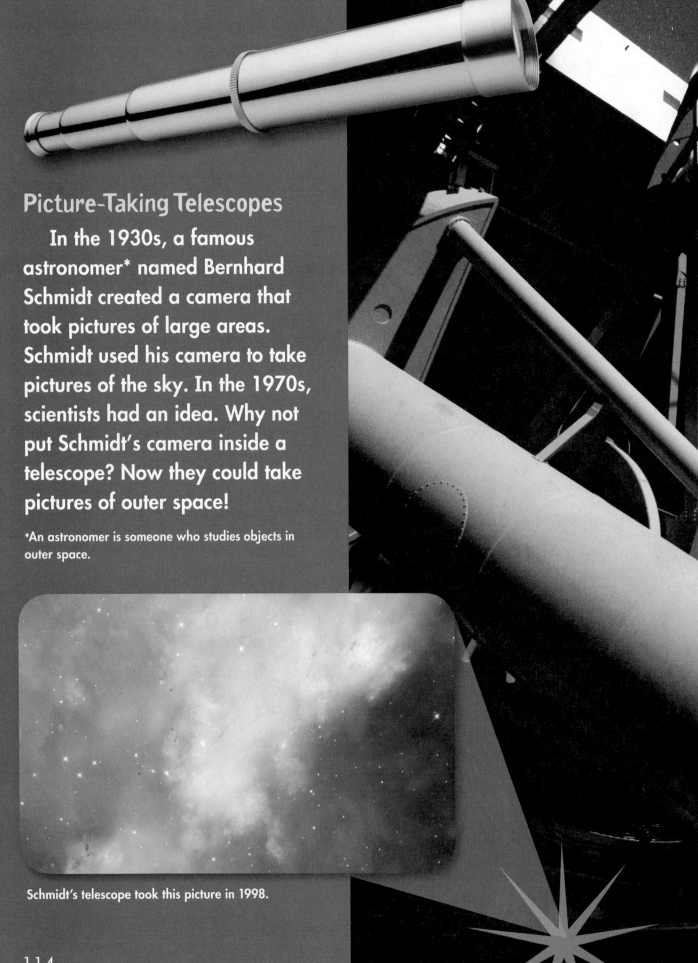

Picture-Taking Telescopes

In the 1930s, a famous astronomer* named Bernhard Schmidt created a camera that took pictures of large areas. Schmidt used his camera to take pictures of the sky. In the 1970s, scientists had an idea. Why not put Schmidt's camera inside a telescope? Now they could take pictures of outer space!

*An astronomer is someone who studies objects in outer space.

Schmidt's telescope took this picture in 1998.

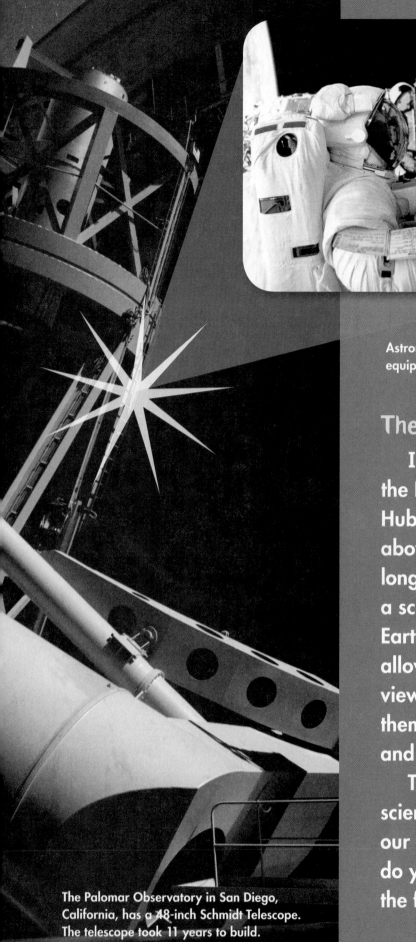

Astronauts go on missions to fix and replace equipment on the Hubble Space Telescope.

The Space Age

In 1990, NASA launched the Hubble Space Telescope. Hubble orbits about 375 miles above Earth. It is over 40 feet long, which is about the size of a school bus! Hubble circles Earth once every 97 minutes. It allows scientists on Earth to view distant stars. And it helps them learn about new planets and other space objects.

Telescopes have helped scientists begin to understand our expanding universe. What do you think they'll find in the future?

The Palomar Observatory in San Diego, California, has a 48-inch Schmidt Telescope. The telescope took 11 years to build.

SPACE

115

SPACESHIPS FROM HOLLYWOOD

by Anthony Ware

What do you think of when someone says "outer space"? Spaceships? Aliens? Evil empires? Many of our ideas about outer space come from television and movies.

Lost in Space was one of the first science fiction television shows.

LOST IN SPACE

In 1965, there was a television series called *Lost in Space*. The show followed the Robinson family. The family went to space to take control of a star system. A spy tried to prevent them from completing their mission. Their ship went off course. The Robinsons were lost in space.

Each week the Robinsons faced new adventures. And they learned how to survive on their new home planet. *Lost in Space* was very popular. Soon other space programs followed.

STAR TREK

One of the most popular science fiction shows of all time was *Star Trek*. The series began in 1966. The show followed the adventures of a crew on board a spaceship in the 23rd century.

(From left to right) Captain Kirk, Mr. Spock, and Dr. McCoy were popular characters on *Star Trek*.

Star Trek used futuristic settings to tell complex stories. Episodes could be about crime, love, or power. Audiences enjoyed watching futuristic people in outer space deal with real problems.

The show took place inside a fictional spaceship called the U.S.S. *Enterprise*. The set design for the *Enterprise* was very realistic. Its engines and control panels were designed to look like a spaceship from the future. The sets made the show seem believable.

A new U.S.S. *Enterprise* was created for *Star Trek: The Next Generation*.

STAR WARS

George Lucas wrote and directed *Star Wars* in 1977. The movie introduced a character named Luke Skywalker. Luke was a Jedi Knight. The Jedi Knights protect weaker star systems in the universe from the giant evil Empire.

Luke Skywalker's journey was like the complex journeys of many heroes before him. He had to learn how to be a Jedi before he faced the evil Darth Vader.

There are six *Star Wars* films. They are some of the most popular movies of all time.

Star Wars was like nothing anyone had ever seen before in movies. The scenes were very realistic. The movie used new computer technology to create special effects and gadgets. *Star Wars* became one of the most popular and successful films about space of all time.

E.T. was a movie that was popular with both children and adults.

E.T. THE EXTRA-TERRESTRIAL

Steven Spielberg's movie *E.T. the Extra-Terrestrial* (EX-tra-tir-RES-tree-uhl) was also a popular movie. It came out in 1982. *Extra-terrestrial* means "from another world."

In the film, an alien named E.T. travels to Earth to learn about our plants. E.T.'s spaceship leaves him, and he meets a ten-year-old boy named Elliot. The two learn how to communicate with each other. Together they create a machine to contact E.T.'s home planet.

E.T. is different from other science fiction films because it happens on Earth. No one flies into space. Instead, creatures from space come to Earth.

THE FUTURE OF SPACE

Images of space have changed throughout the years. Some have been humorous. And some have been serious. Technology has helped make television series and movies about space seem more realistic. But one thing remains the same—they're all out of this world!

WHAT DO YOU THINK?

How is E.T. different from other shows about space?

Searching the UNIVERSE

by Graham Roth • Illustrated by Matthew Trueman

Brian wondered about the universe every day.
He wanted to be an astronomer like his hero, Galileo.
He talked about astronomy all the time. His family
called him little Galileo.

When Brian was ten his grandfather gave him
a telescope.

"Enjoy exploring the galaxy," Grandpa said.

At night Brian studied the sky through his telescope.
He wrote about what he saw in his notebook. He
compared his notes with the poster of the galaxy on
his bedroom wall.

Sometimes Brian drew pictures of planets and star formations. He dreamed about one day discovering a new planet.

One evening, the moon was in its last phase. It was a quarter moon. Brian was looking for planets through his telescope. Suddenly he saw a new object near the moon. *Could it be a new planet?* he wondered. *It's a scientific fact that more than 155 planets are outside of our solar system.*

But he knew that his telescope could not see that far into space. "That looks like a new planet in our solar system!" he said.

"Mom, Dad! I found a new planet!" he shouted. "You've got to see this!"

His mother was working in the basement. His father was in the kitchen. They couldn't hear him. Brian ran to grab his sketch pad. He wanted to draw a picture of what he saw.

"My first scientific discovery!" Brian said to himself.

Brian went back to his telescope and cleaned the lens.

126

Just then, Grandpa poked his head into Brian's room. "Did I hear you made a discovery?" he asked. "Let me have a look."

Grandpa looked through the telescope. He scanned the night sky looking for something unusual.

"Where?" Grandpa asked, squinting. "All I see is a bunch of stars and the moon."

"It's near the moon," Brian insisted. "It has an orange glow."

127

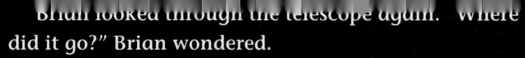

Brian looked through the telescope again. "Where did it go?" Brian wondered.

"Don't be disappointed," Grandpa said. "I think you saw a lunar eclipse.* It can make the moon look orange."

"An eclipse!" Now Mom had come into room.

"But a lunar eclipse only happens during a full moon," Brian said. "The moon is in the last quarter."

"I think you've been looking at the universe for too long. It's time for lights out," said Mom.

*When the moon passes through the Earth's shadow, the Earth blocks the sun's light, so the moon is dark.

Our Solar System

What did I see then? Brian wondered as he got ready for bed. He tried to sleep, but it was no use.

"I might as well look again," he mumbled. Brian walked over to the window to look through his telescope.

As he searched the sky, Brian thought about all the new planets in the universe waiting to be discovered. Brian knew that telescopes were getting more powerful all the time.

Someday, Brian thought, *I'll work with the most powerful telescopes in the world.* Brian looked through the telescope for the orange globe. He couldn't find it. Everything in the galaxy appeared as it did on his poster. Then he took out his sketch pad. He drew the planet he had seen earlier.

The next morning Grandpa burst into Brian's room. "They discovered a new planet!" he shouted, waving a newspaper.

Brian sat up in bed. His eyes tried to focus on the newspaper that Grandpa had.

"This picture looks like the one you drew," Grandpa said, comparing the newspaper to Brian's drawing.

Brian read that the planet was almost ten billion miles from the sun. *My telescope can't see that far,* Brian thought. *Or can it?*

Brian's new planet

What Do You Think?
Why did Grandpa compare Brian's drawings with the pictures in the newspaper?

The Sounds of Space

A phone call to Japan, a soccer game in Germany, and music from Brazil all have one thing in common. They all have traveled into outer space. Every day, satellites in space receive and send millions of signals from telephones, televisions, and radios here on Earth.

Satellites circle Earth like huge antennas. They allow us almost instantly to see and hear things from thousands of miles away. But does that mean that space is filled with sounds from Earth? No.

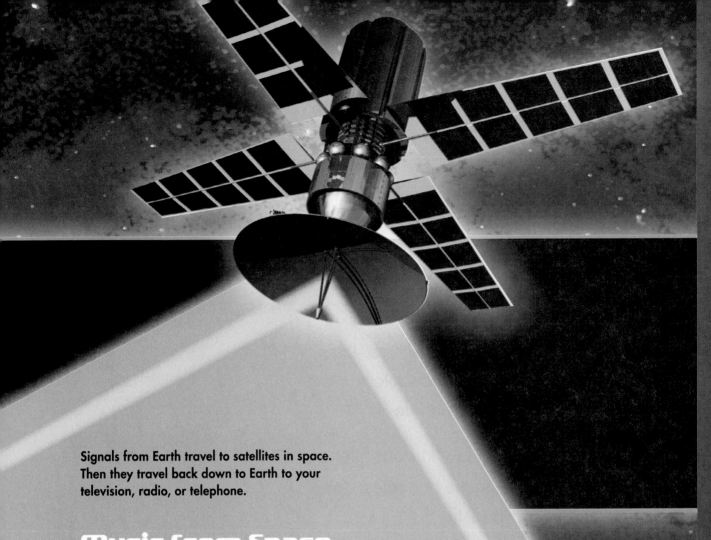

Signals from Earth travel to satellites in space.
Then they travel back down to Earth to your
television, radio, or telephone.

Music from Space

You cannot hear any sounds in space.
But there are radio waves. NASA (National
Aeronautics and Space Administration) has
recorded many radio waves from different
planets in our solar system. They then take these
radio waves and change them into sounds. It
may only be a whistling or hissing sound. But for
the people at NASA, this is music to their ears.

4 you 2 Do

Word Play

This week we explored space. Use some of this week's vocabulary words to create a new movie title.

Use the words below in your titles.

**galaxy   universe   telescope
scientific   futuristic**

Making Connections

What kind of space movie or TV show do you think Brian would like? Explain.

On Paper

What do you think it would be like to travel in space?

Glossary

a·chieve (ə chēv′), *VERB.* to carry out to a successful end; accomplish; do: *We achieved our goal of winning the game.* **a·chieved, a·chiev·ing.**

ap·ply (ə plī′), *VERB.* to set to work and stick to it: *She applied herself to learning to play the piano.*

ap·pre·ci·ate (ə prē′ shē āt), *VERB.* to think highly of; recognize the worth of; value; enjoy: *We appreciate his hard work.*

awk·ward (ȯk′ ward), *ADJECTIVE.* embarrassing: *He asked me such an awkward question that I did not know how to reply.*

bar·ri·er (bar′ ē ər), *NOUN.* something that stands in the way: *The barrier kept people off the railroad tracks.*

cir·cum·stance (sėr′kəm stans), *NOUN.* a condition that goes along with some fact or event: *What were the circumstances of the accident?* PL. **cir·cum·stan·ces.**

com·plex (kəm pleks′ or kom′ pleks), *ADJECTIVE.* 1. made up of a number of parts that work together: *A computer is a complex device.* 2. hard to understand: *The instructions for our new computer game were so complex that they were hard to follow.*

a in hat	ō in open	sh in she
ā in age	ȯ in all	th in thin
â in care	ô in order	⊤H in then
ä in far	oi in oil	zh in measure
e in let	ou in out	ə = a in about
ē in equal	u in cup	ə = e in taken
ėr in term	u̇ in put	ə = i in pencil
i in it	ü in rule	ə = o in lemon
ī in ice	ch in child	ə = u in circus
o in hot	ng in long	

GLOSSARY

con·vic·tion (kən vik′ shən), NOUN. a strong belief: *It's my conviction that hard work leads to success.*

de·ter·mined (di tėr′ mənd), ADJECTIVE. with your mind made up: *Her determined look showed that she had decided what to do.*

de·vise (di vīz′), VERB. to think up some way of doing something; invent: *The kids are trying to devise a way to earn money during vacation.* **de·vised, de·vis·ing.**

dis·ting·uish (dis ting′ gwish), VERB. to see the differences between things; tell apart: *Can you distinguish frogs from toads?* **dis·tin·guish·es, dis·tin·guished, dis·tin·guish·ing.**

ef·fi·cient (ə fish′ ənt), ADJECTIVE. able to do something without waste of time, energy, or materials; capable: *An efficient worker makes good use of his or her time.*

fur·i·ous (fyùr′ ē əs), ADJECTIVE. very angry: *The owner of the home was furious when she saw the broken window.*

fu·tur·is·tic (fyü′ chə ris′ tik), ADJECTIVE. of or like something in the future: *At the auto show, John saw a futuristic car.*

gal·ax·y (gal′ ək sē), NOUN. a group of billions of stars forming one system: *The Earth and the sun are in the Milky Way galaxy.*

a in hat	ō in open	sh in she
ā in age	ȯ in all	th in thin
â in care	ô in order	ŦH in then
ä in far	oi in oil	zh in measure
e in let	ou in out	ə = a in about
ē in equal	u in cup	ə = e in taken
ėr in term	ù in put	ə = i in pencil
i in it	ü in rule	ə = o in lemon
ī in ice	ch in child	ə = u in circus
o in hot	ng in long	

head·way (hed′ wā′), NOUN. progress: *Medical science has made much headway in fighting disease.*

hur·dle (hėr′ dl), NOUN. something that stands in the way; difficulty: *My parents' consent was the last hurdle before I could join the football team.* PL. **hur·dles.**

im·mi·gra·tion (im′ ə grā′ shən), NOUN. coming into a foreign country to live there: *There has been immigration to the United States from many countries.*

in·ter·na·tion·al (in′ tər nash′ ə nəl), ADJECTIVE. between or among two or more countries: *Ben likes to watch international soccer.*

mo·del (mod′ l), *ADJECTIVE.* 1. being a small copy of something: *His hobby is making model airplanes.* 2. just right or perfect; ideal: *He tried very hard to be a model student.*

oc·cu·pa·tion (ok′ yə pā′ shən), *NOUN.* the work someone does regularly or to earn a living: *Jill's chosen occupation is nursing.* PL. **oc·cu·pa·tions.**

per·se·ver·ance (pėr′ sə vir′ əns), *NOUN.* sticking to a purpose or an aim; never giving up what you have set out to do: *By perseverance, I finally learned to swim.*

a in hat	ō in open	sh in she
ā in age	ȯ in all	th in thin
â in care	ô in order	ŦH in then
ä in far	oi in oil	zh in measure
e in let	ou in out	ə = a in about
ē in equal	u in cup	ə = e in taken
ėr in term	u̇ in put	ə = i in pencil
i in it	ü in rule	ə = o in lemon
ī in ice	ch in child	ə = u in circus
o in hot	ng in long	

per·son·al·i·ty (pėr′ sə nal′ ə tē), *NOUN.* an individual quality that makes someone different from another person: *Her warm, friendly personality makes her popular.*

pro·cras·ti·nate (prō kras′ tə nāt), *VERB.* to put things off until later; delay: *It's not a good idea to procrastinate when you have a project to do.* **pro·cras·ti·nates, pro·cras·ti·nat·ed, pro·cras·ti·nat·ing.**

pro·gress (prog′ res), *NOUN.* the act or process of moving forward: *We made rapid progress on our trip to Utah.*

sci·en·tif·ic (sī′ ən tif′ ik), *ADJECTIVE.* using the facts and laws of science: *The poster of the solar system helped him learn scientific facts about the planets.*

sug·gest (səg jest′ or sə jest′), *VERB.* to bring up an idea; propose: *She suggested a swim, and we all agreed.* **sug·gest·ed, sug·gest·ing.**

tel·e·scope (tel′ ə skōp), *NOUN*. a device you look through that makes things far away seem to be nearer and larger: *Objects in space are studied with telescopes.*

tim·id (tim′ id), *ADJECTIVE*. easily frightened; shy: *The timid child was afraid of singing in front of the audience.*

u·ni·verse (yü′ nə vėrs′), *NOUN*. everything there is, including all space and matter: *Our planet is a very tiny part of the universe.*

a in hat	ō in open	sh in she
ā in age	ȯ in all	th in thin
â in care	ô in order	ŦH in then
ä in far	oi in oil	zh in measure
e in let	ou in out	ə = a in about
ē in equal	u in cup	ə = e in taken
ėr in term	u̇ in put	ə = i in pencil
i in it	ü in rule	ə = o in lemon
ī in ice	ch in child	ə = u in circus
o in hot	ng in long	

Acknowledgments

Text

Every effort has been made to locate the copyright owner of material reproduced in this component. Omissions brought to our attention will be corrected in subsequent editions. Grateful acknowledgment is made to the following for copyrighted material.

26 Marian Reiner, Literary Agent "74th Street" by Myra Cohn Livingston from *The Malibu and Other Poems.* Copyright © 1972 by Myra Cohn Livingston. All rights renewed and reserved. Used by permission of Marian Reiner.

28 Sheree Fitch "Ladder to the Sky" by Sheree Fitch from *Toes in My Nose, and Other Poems.* Copyright © 1987 by Sheree Fitch. Used by permission of the author.

Illustrations

18–24, Cover Terry Widener; **26, 28** Laura Huliska-Beith; **46–52** Jim Steck; **88–94** Judith Du Four Love; **124–130, 142** Matthew Trueman.

Photographs

Every effort has been made to secure permission and provide appropriate credit for photographic material. The publisher deeply regrets any omission and pledges to correct errors called to its attention in subsequent editions.

Unless otherwise acknowledged, all photographs are the property of Pearson Education, Inc.

Photo locators denoted as follows: Top (T), Center (C), Bottom (B), Left (L), Right (R), Background (Bkgd)

Cover (CR) Lucy Nicholson/Corbis, (Back) Nick Vedros & Assoc/Getty Images, (BR) Roger Ball/Roger Ball Photography; **3** (T) Getty Images, (CL) James L. Amos/Corbis, (B) AF archive/Alamy; **4** (CR) ©Myrleen Pearson/PhotoEdit, (TR) Getty Images; **5** (C) John Lund/Getty Images; **6** (TL) Getty Images, (CR) The Granger Collection, NY; **7** (C) AP/Wide World Photos, (BR) Mike Abrahams/Alamy, (T) The Granger Collection, NY; **8** (BC) Getty Images, (CR, BR) The Granger Collection, NY; **9** (TR) B.W. Kilburn/Corbis, (R) Getty Images; **10** (BR) Bettmann/Corbis, (TR) Jim Ruymen/Corbis; **11** (C) James L. Amos/Corbis; **12** (T) Suzanne Mapes/AP/Wide World Photos; **13** (BR) Mike Abrahams/Alamy, (CC) Colin McPherson/Corbis, (BL) Warner Bros./Zuma/Zuma Press, Inc.; **14** (B) Henryk Sadura/Shutterstock, (TL) Photographs and Prints Division/The New York Public Library/Astor, Lenox, and Tilden Foundations/Schomburg Center for Research in Black Culture; **15** (T) Cynthia Johnson/Getty Images; **16** (TL) AP/Wide World Photos, (TR) Bettmann/Corbis; **17** (CC) Bettmann/Corbis, (BR) Corbis; **30** (BR) Getty Images; **31** (C) Zigy Kaluzny/Getty Images; **32** (C) Bettmann/Corbis, (T) DK Limited/Corbis, (CC) Getty Images; **33** (C, B) Bettmann/Corbis, (C) Didrik Johnck/Corbis, (R) Gurinder Osan/AP/Wide World Photos, (CR) John Van Hasselt/Corbis, (TR) William Whitehurst/Corbis; **34** (C) Bettmann/Corbis; **35** (BR) ©Michael Freeman/Corbis, (TL) The Granger Collection, NY; **36** (R) Bettmann/Corbis, (CL) Library of Congress; **37** (R) DK Limited/Corbis; **38** (CL) Aaron J. Walker/AP/Wide World Photos, (C) Getty Images; **39** (CR) ©Royalty-Free/Corbis; **40** (C) ©Royalty-Free/Corbis, (TC) Getty Images, (TR) Raffles Hospital, HO/AP/Wide World Photos; **41** (Bkgd) ©John Branscombe/Alamy Images, (R) ©Royalty-Free/Corbis, (TC) National Air and Space Museum, Smithsonian Institution; **42** (TC) AP/Wide World Photos, (B) Bettmann/Corbis; **43** (CR) Getty Images, (C) Lon C. Dhiel/PhotoEdit, (TR) Preston Gannaway/AP/Wide World Photos; **44** (TL) Andrew Lichtenstein/Corbis, (C) Lucas Jackson/Corbis; **45** (TR) J. Scott Applewhite/AP/Wide World Photos, (TC) William Whitehurst/Corbis; **54** (B) David Keaton/Corbis; **55** (CL) Bettmann/Corbis, (C) Didrik Johnck/Corbis, (CR) Gurinder Osan/AP/Wide World Photos, (CC) John Van Hasselt/Corbis; **57** (C) Jim Cummins/Getty Images; **58** (B) David Ball/Corbis, (TR, TL) Getty Images; **59** (C) Lucy Nicholson/Corbis; **60** (TL, BR) Getty Images, (TR) Najlah Feanny/Corbis; **61** (B) Getty Images, (TR) Lewis Wickes Hine/Corbis, (TL) Shannon Stapleton/Corbis; **62** (C) Lucy Nicholson/Corbis; **63** (T) Getty Images; **64** (BR) James Nielsen/Getty Images, (C) Marcelo del Pozo/Corbis; **65** (B) Getty Images; **66** (T) ©George Wong/AP/Wide World Photos; **67** (BR) Lucy Nicholson/Corbis; **68** (T) Jennifer E. Pottheiser/Getty Images; **69** (BL) Lucy Nicholson/Corbis, (TR) Wilson Chu/Corbis; **70** (TL) ©Bettmann/Corbis, (C, B) Getty Images; **71** (CC, B) Getty Images, (TR) Jupiter Images; **72** (CC) Frances Benjamin Johnston Collection/Library of Congress, (TR, TL) Getty Images; **73** (BC) ©Royalty-Free/Corbis, (T) Getty Images, (CC) Owaki - Kulla/Corbis; **74** (T, B) Getty Images, (CC) Photo Collection Alexander Alland, Sr./Corbis; **75** (C, BL) Getty Images, (B) Jupiter Images; **76** (T) Getty Images, (CC) Vincenzo Lombardo/Getty Images; **77** (BR) Getty Images, (CC) Klaus Hackenberg/Corbis; **78** (C) David Ball/Corbis; **79** (C) ©Lawrence Migdale; **80** (C) Claudia Adams/Danita Delimont, Agent; **81** (C) Tony Freeman/PhotoEdit; **82** (BR) Getty Images; **83** Myrleen Pearson; **84** (CR) ©Amazing Kids!, (C) ©Jake Lyell/Heifer International., (B) Photolibrary Group, Inc.; **85** (BC) ©Geoff Oliver Bugbee/Heifer International.; **86** (CR) ©Ariel Skelley/Corbis; **87** (TL) ©Danielle Nowitz/Corbis, (TR) ©Martin Shields/Alamy Images; **88** (C) ©Amazing Kids!; **96** (BR) Heifer International.; **97** (C, B) Heifer International.; **98** (BR) ©Darcy Keifel/Heifer International., (C) ©Jake Lyell/Heifer International.; **99** (BR) ©Geoff Oliver Bugbee/Heifer International.; **100** (C) ©Darcy Keifel/Heifer International., (BL) ©Darcy Kiefel/Heifer International.; **101** (BR) ©Darcy Kiefel/Heifer International., (TR) Heifer International.; **102** (C) Heifer International.; **103** (TL) Heifer International.; **104** (B) Photolibrary Group, Inc.; **105** (T) ©Eric Fowke/PhotoEdit, Inc.; **106** (C) ©Myrleen Pearson/PhotoEdit; **107** (BR) ©Jupiterimages/Comstock Images/Alamy; **108** (BC) ©Geoff Oliver Bugbee/Heifer International.; **109** (C) PhotoAlto/Getty Images; **110** (TL) Getty Images, (T) Jet Propulsion Laboratory /NASA Image Exchange; **111** AF archive/Alamy; **112** (BR) ©Charles C. Place/Getty Images, (C) Getty Images; **113** (TR) ©Bettmann/Corbis, (TC) Jet Propulsion Laboratory /NASA Image Exchange; **114** (T) Getty Images, (BL) Jet Propulsion Laboratory /NASA Image Exchange, Palomar Observatory; **115** (TR, TC) Getty Images; **116** (C) Digital Art/Corbis; **117** Moviestore Collection Ltd/Alamy; **118** (TC) United Archives GmbH/Alamy; **118–119** AF archive/Alamy; **120** (T) Lucasfilm Ltd./20th Century Fox Film Corp./Photofest; **121** (CL) Lucasfilm Ltd./20th Century Fox Film Corp./Photofest, (CR) LucasFilm/20th Century Fox/The Kobal Collection; **122** (T, CL) Terry Chostner/Bruce McBroom/Universal Pictures/Photofest; **123** (B) Roger Ball/Roger Ball Photography; **132** (B) Dean C. Kalmantis/Images/Corbis, (T) Getty Images; **133** (T, BR) Getty Images; **134** (TR) Gregory MacNicol/Photo Researchers, Inc.; **136** (TR) Getty Images; **137** (CR) Getty Images; **138** (CR) Getty Images; **139** (B) Getty Images; **140** (TR) ©AbleStock/Index Open, (BC) Najlah Feanny/Corbis; **143** (TR) ©Inmagine/Alamy.

144